DRIVING W/ CRAZY

LIVING WITH MADNESS

JACK HENRY

PUNK ★ HOSTAGE ★ PRESS

DRIVING W/CRAZY
LIVING WITH MADNESS

Editor
Puma Perl

Introduction
Rob Plath

Cover Illustration
Billy Burgos

Special Thanks
Jack Varnell
Diana Rose
Gillian Anderson

Author would like to express gratitude to the following publications for publishing items that are included herein: **smoking typewriter, horror sleaze trash, hobo camp, raven cage, marie lecrivain, dissident voice, ariel chart, rye whiskey review.**

Punk Hostage Press
Hollywood, California

for Kelly, as always
&
my father, obviously
&
Cameron, my son

introduction

I'm so happy to write this introduction for Jack Henry's newest poetry book Driving w/Crazy, which will be published this year by the great Punk Hostage Press in California. To be honest, I usually dread when someone asks me to write an introduction, a review, or even a blurb for their books because much too often I don't connect with the writing, or don't like the writer's craft very much, or both, etc., and any of those tasks becomes very forced and like hard work, but with this book, it's not only a simple task; it's pure delight I'm actually excited to pen the introduction for Jack Henry.

And I'm writing this the first day of the new year, January 1, 2021, and it's nice to start off the new beginning with something like this. And I must say this, after the hell of 2020, this book is definitely something that should exist and is worth owning. Because if we look through the lens of the terrible, unprecedented, previous year, one thing it should teach us is not to waste time on dumb shit, to put it bluntly. I think for many of us, we were granted, whether we wanted it or not, what Hemingway called a "bullshit detector." And this book is quite the opposite of bullshit. No alarms go off with this collection. Actually, come to think of it, Robert Frost was wrong, in a way, that "nothing gold can stay." I strongly predict this book will remain and it is gold if there ever was any.

I loved that these poems were a rehearsal for Jack Henry's own potential madness and future death. This whole work very much reminded me of the memories and emotion in Allen Ginsberg's long poem for his mother Naomi, "Kaddish." How Jack mixes memories both sweet and painful while the horrifying backdrop of mental illness, physical illness, and death looms there throughout the work. And that we all will, as Jack so perfectly puts it, sit in "the same chair" one day. Whether it be the chair of madness or illness or death.

I loved the SAMENESS theme in this book, and how a similar fate awaits the son who possesses the "same giant head" as the father. But who also cannot always communicate with his father-twin. These particular poems partly remind me of what Franz Kafka once wrote in a letter to his own father: "My writing was all about you; all I did there, after all, was to bemoan what I could not bemoan upon your breast." There's definitely a feeling of this throughout the book. It's powerful and melancholic and pure poetry.

In general, each of these poems are a fragile yet sturdy mini-film of family and the sweetness and pain of growing up, and facing adulthood demons, captured by the beautiful command of the alphabet the author possesses. They are a well selected inventory of inner pictures that could not stay locked up—it is the past, not so much "scraped through" as the Jack writes in one piece, but rather fragments of the past that are scooped from his very shape, which were "buried in bone," as the author so succinctly puts it, and carved, very well-carved indeed.

At times the poems remind one of a precious vinyl record that suddenly is skipping back and forth between the grooves of loss and sweetness with memorable lines such as "madness doesn't ask permission" and "now my father captains his ship toward Heaven's forever."

One of the most moving poems is the one when Jack imagines he will "break his father free" from his confinement in the home, as well as from his failing shape and live a tender moment and these poems actually do that. I see these as little magic poetry time-machines that save his father, and Jack too, and all of us.

Another one of the poems that moved me the most is the one where he tells his father, who is well aware of his imminent end at this point, that "we all dying just at different speeds," and it sums of the book for me. It's back to SAMENESS. We all get to the same place eventually. The positions will switch. In this case, the father becomes the helpless child, the son becomes more like the father. The pain of the powerbase switching is horrible and gut wrenching. That terrible chair awaits us all. But while we are here some of us will be courageous enough to bear witness and suffer and write poems too, sometimes a whole book of them that won't go away. This book is one of them.

Rob Plath,
author of numerous poetry collections,
including *Bellyful of Anarchy (Epic Rites Press)*
January 2021

editor's note

When Jack Henry told me he wanted me to edit his book my gut reaction was twofold: honored and terrified.

We have been arguing for the last decade, if not longer, about which of us writes better poems; he insists that I do, I stand firm in my belief that his work is superior.

I think back to 2009 when we were both working on our first full-length collections. We exchanged manuscripts. I read his near-final draft of *the Patience of Monuments* and immediately tossed my unfinished manuscript in the garbage. I would have set it on fire, if not for the smoke detector. I'd have shot it if I'd had a gun.

How could I possibly edit Jack Henry's book?

And then...I realize that without Jack, I might not have tossed my mediocre draft and subsequently written a collection that even I think is sort of okay. I don't know if he's sometimes my muse or I'm sometimes his, but what has become clear is that we are poets and colleagues, and as such one cannot be better than the other because we are more than our poems. We are the ways we see, hear, and envision; we are the matter in our memories, in our DNA, in our energies.

At the start of the pandemic, before publication was even discussed, Jack was my one of my primary lifelines, both of us in our bunkers, 3,000 miles away, poetry and daily check-ins bringing us closer to human contact.

Once I stepped out of my own way, I agreed to edit Jack's book, and despite what I said about the soul of poets being impossible to measure, if pressed, I will still insist he's the better writer.

But that's okay, because why would I want to be the best in the room? Putting ego aside, what would I learn? I loved working on this book with Jack, his honesty and vulnerability allowing me into his life and his truth. One of his strengths in writing about people is his ability to look into others in relation to their worlds and their hearts, with and without his presence.

He has the courage to open the wounds that will never quite heal, but that may hurt a little less, in time.

Thank you, Jack Henry and Iris Berry and Punk Hostage Press for trusting me to be part of this process. For a book editing rookie like myself, I could not imagine a better experience. I didn't plan it this way, but writing this note on the first day of 2021 is a great start to what I hope will be a year filled with renewed hope, love, and poetry.

Puma Perl, *editor*
01/01/2021

contents

AND YOU MAY FIND YOURSELF

    LIVING IN A SHOTGUN SHACK

AND YOU MAY FIND YOURSELF

    IN ANOTHER PART OF THE WORLD

AND YOU MAY FIND YOURSELF

    BEHIND THE WHEEL OF A LARGE AUTOMOBILE

AND YOU MAY FIND YOURSELF

    IN A BEAUTIFUL HOUSE, WITH A BEAUTIFUL WIFE

AND YOU MAY ASK YOURSELF,

    "WELL...HOW DID I GET HERE?"

Once in a Lifetime, Talking Heads

cartoon memory playground

madness strikes
when we're not looking,
when we sit crying
in the last pew of a church.

madness comes calling
when we wash our umbrellas,
when a murder of crows
suddenly flies by.

madness doesn't ask for permission
from diamond starred haloes,
madness does not need
anything to survive.

madness sits waiting
in flimsy silk stockings,
in the back of a cupboard
where all the spiders hide.

madness makes normal
feel like we're crazy,
makes living feel deadly,
makes breathing a lie.

madness is magic
for all the wrong reasons.
i lived with that crazy
all of my life.

and when the red pill stops working
and they always stop working,
madness will kill you
with a wink and a sigh.

8mm memories

my mind's awash
with 8mm memories.
faded and fragile film
winds through
a clattering projector.
images flicker and dance,
magic light
in the back of my skull.

sister, mother,
and
father
whisper through memory,

ghosts against the grain.

there is laughter and joy,
tears and anger.
impending death
makes all memory
brighter, stronger,

and i want
to capture
every single
one.

my father

as a kid i always stood / in the shadow of my father /

baseball games at Dodger Stadium / when he yelled at anyone / in front
of us / who yelled at me for being too loud /

warm days down on the docks / adjacent to San Pedro / as he
sanded down the boat / and i chased little crabs littering / boulders along
the shore /

summer days / fetching beers as he watched tv / as i ran in and out /
of the house / endlessly /

the time / he didn't recognize me / during a 5150 lock-down /

late at night / when i heard my mother crying /
he was coming home late / again /

my father is complicated but i guess we all are / complicated /

life is complicated /

rules don't change / between father and son /
except / at some point /
a son grows up / moves out / moves on /
and / becomes a father /

i have a daughter / now /

something is missing / something not quite right /
but there is something
i cannot understand / or translate /
or put to paper /

my daughter moved away / i know she will be back /
she told me she would be back / i count on that /
she is a part of my history / just as i am /
a part of my parents' history /

but something is missing /

i took a DNA test to prove / who i am / where i am from /
what i am about / as if my very existence had no proof /
as if a glob of spit will tell me everything / i need to know /

as my father grows older / i watch intently / knowing one-day
i will be in the same place / the same space / the same chair /
fighting against and losing against / time itself /

at 80 he's lived a while /

at 55 i am not sure i will make it that far /

finding the strength to lead my father home

he's an old man
living in the past
and clinging to a future
that shortens
every day.

i'd like to say i know him
but i don't.
i didn't really try.
i could never communicate with him.
words failed me,
i could not speak
without falling.

time is still with us
aloof and fleeting
but here,

for a moment.

we share the same eyes,
same nose,
same giant head that could be
used as advertising space.

we share everything.

my reflection is 80.
his is 55.
he is dying.
i am barely here.

i think of moments
at the boatyard,
walking the docks in Newport Harbor
on Saturday mornings,
sailing to Catalina,
watching Navy football.

there are still minutes left,
a precious few,
but i cannot face another breath
without my father
in my life.

he faced his demons
every day.
sometimes he would win…

i face my own demons.
some built by stick and stone,
some found buried in bone.

my heart beats faster
as i think,
as i write,

as i find the strength
to lead my father home.

mother stands
on the front porch
of my childhood home
and waves brightly
as i walk off to my first day
of first grade.

i am terrified.

my father sits in
a wheelchair
in his room, staring
at a wall. my footsteps
echo as i walk toward him.

school is big and scary.
lots of kids i do not know.
some glare at me,
mostly i am ignored.
the teacher seems nice
but everything is new
and different.

a nurse gives me an update
about my father's medication,
his care, how things work on a
day-to-day basis.
i sit with him as we wait
for breakfast.

at recess i make a friend.
we remain friends until i
move to Orange County
in the middle of fourth grade.

> *my father introduces*
> *me to Bill, his roommate.*
> *they are fast friends after*
> *two days. my father*
> *says he will take care*
> *of Bill. and the others.*

my mother asks me about
first grade and i say
it's a little frightening but
i will be okay.
i mention that i'd
rather be home
with her.

and 51 years later
my father says the same thing.

driving w/crazy

my mother waved
as my father
& i drove away.

as a kid
i had the backseat
all to myself.
bumping around,
sliding
from side to side as
he made a turn.
left to right,
right to left.

as my mother
faded from sight
i lost my shit.
a six-year-old
in the backseat
of a Corvair
screaming
for his mother.

even then i knew
driving w/crazy
would scar me for life.

as he turned back toward the house
i settled down.
the following
Saturday i made it
a little bit farther.

that's how it worked.
every day
i got a little farther
down the road.

then you find the road
really never
ends when you're
driving w/crazy.

the time i remember best

I grew up in a nothing town, in a nothing part of the state, in a nothing part of the world; a life no different than those around me.

As memory serves, my father worked as a banker in downtown Los Angeles. In the late sixties/early seventies I have no idea what the traffic would have been to travel twenty-three miles point-to-point but nowadays traffic is nothing sort of pure nightmare. However, traffic must have been relatively decent as my mother would drive me to my father's place of business, a bank near 7th & Figueroa, and drop me off so I could go to baseball games with my father at Dodger Stadium.

Times were different then, trusting a 7-8-year-old waking into a bank didn't register a second thought. Besides, I was big for my age and tough. Well sort of tough. At least in my mind.

My father's eyes exploded with light when I pushed through the big glass door of the bank. He would show me around, introduce me to people, expressing nothing but pride and joy. This is the father I always remember when times grew dark. Even years later, when I showed up at his place of business, he expressed the same enthusiasm. By then I considered myself a grown man, all of 16, and my interest lay in the receptionist up front with the short skirt, rather than what the old man did for a living. I never really knew what his *job* entailed and back then a son didn't ask.

Often times when my mother dropped me off, I would have to wait in reception or on a big chair in my father's office. Some days the wait was longer than others. If he needed more than a few minutes he let me go outside, onto the streets of Los Angeles. Memory suggests I ran crazy through back alleys, down main streets, and into speakeasies chasing beautiful dames, but, most likely, I stood on the corner staring up at tall buildings.

Downtown Los Angeles was a great wonder to me back when I was little. And it still is as an adult. Massive buildings and a billion miles of freeways, and so many people; I thought the whole world was just like Los Angeles.

When my father finally finished work, he would come find me. If I was alone staring up at tall buildings, he would stare up too. He would always wait until I was ready to go, and I was always ready to go when it came to going to a baseball game.

With baseball mitt in hand, I would struggle to contain my enthusiasm. I loved baseball. Everything about it. The smell, the sound, home runs, strikeouts. Everything. And the 10-15-minute drive from 7th & Figueroa to Dodger Stadium felt like a day and a half.

The seats my father's company owned were great. First base side, 10 or so rows off the field. When I screamed, I knew the players heard me. And the Dodgers always won when I sat at field level. Always. Except once. I never knew why we moved our seats for just one game but we ended up at the top of Dodger Stadium, third base side. A million miles away. Sadly, the Dodgers lost to the Atlanta Braves. Of course, I blamed the location of the seats and my inability to yell at the Braves.

But that night we sat at field level. The best! Hot dog, soda, sitting with my father; life just didn't get better than that moment.

For me a baseball game is church. There are customs and ceremonies, specific things that take place. When they announced the line-up, I wrote the names down. Steve Garvey at First Base, Ron Cey at Third, Davey Lopes at Second; man, they could play! I stood solemnly for the National Anthem, careful to remove my hat and place my hand over my heart. During school I rebelled and kept my hand down, but not at a baseball game. Never at a baseball game. Then you scream, Beat Army! And then you cheer the first pitch no matter how lousy a throw.

The last ritual was to say hello to the people around you and my father knew everyone or, at least, said hello to everyone. He loved a crowd and groups of people.

On this particular night the crowd was loud. Really loud! And being loud became a big part of my experience. Like I said, so close the ballplayers could hear you. And I did my damnedest to make sure they heard me.

The guys in the seats front of me didn't take to kindly to some dumbass kid SCREAMING in their ears. One of them said as much.

"Hey kid! Whyn't you shut the fuck up?"

He might as well have slapped me across the face, spit in my soda, and knocked my hot dog to the ground. I was devastated.

Tears came hard and fast; they always did in those days. Grown-ups called me tender hearted, the kids at school called me worse.

That night my father watched it happen and he let those guys have it. Never in my life had I heard my father cheer as loud for the Dodgers! He screamed, *let's go Dodgers* and *pitchers got a rubber arm*, and all the other stupid shit kids scream at baseball games.

I don't remember much after that. Win, lose; who cared? I didn't.

The guys in front of us left after another inning or two after my father and I screamed without stop. A few people around us that overheard the whole thing joined in, screaming and chanting. I beamed the rest of the night.

We probably got home late and I probably fell asleep in the car. But I know I couldn't wait for the next game, and there was a next game, but not like that one. That game was the best, the kind of baseball game that becomes a memory, not because of the game, but because of a father that stood up for his kid, and lost his voice in the process.

Rotten Jimmy

during the summer
between 3rd & 4th grade,
my friends & i
would walk down
to the Plunge,
the big swimming pool at
Verdugo High School.

mom would give me
four quarters,
enough for entrance & a locker.
she'd pack a sandwich,
cookies & an apple.
always an apple.

every time we went to the Plunge
the big kids would terrorize us.
especially Rotten Jimmy.
we never knew his real name.
we gave him that one.

Rotten Jimmy
would punch you in the ass
if you moved too slow
getting out of the pool.

one day he took it a little too far.
he punched me in the ass
as i pulled from the pool.
i froze, turned & kicked him
square in the face, breaking his nose with a pop,
one that everyone heard.

i got banned from the Plunge.
had to answer to mom and
waited for my father to come home.

through tears
& blind rage,
i told my story.

my father took me & my sister
for ice cream.
three scoops.
all in.

late fall Rotten Jimmy got arrested
for selling speed to kids
at Verdugo High School.
my dad showed me his mug shot
posted in the local newspaper,
his nose bent & broken.

i smiled to myself,
hoping he'd always think of me
whenever he looked
in a mirror.

Richard & Johnny

Richard and Johnny
were best friends
and, most days,
hated each other.

Richard lived next door to me.
Johnny down the street
in a big house with a dirt yard
next to an alley.

both boys were older than me
by a couple of years,
yet they let me tag along,
mostly because i kept up
with their expletive laden language
and stood roughly the same height.

we never did much, other than
hang out on the street
under the concrete lampposts.
play baseball
and street hockey.

when the streetlights blinked on
we would go home.

one hot random day
Johnny and Richard got into it.
a screaming match
about something stupid.
Richard held out a pocket knife,
promising to stab Johnny
if he didn't shut *the fuck* up.

Johnny removed his belt as a weapon,
then grabbed a kitchen knife,
finally retrieved his father's .38 revolver.

'i'm gonna kill you,' he screamed
and we believed him,
as he stood on his front porch
waving his father's .38 revolver around.

Johnny's mother finally
broke away from her soaps,
lumbered out onto the porch,
saw the gun,
and punched Johnny
in the ear;

Johnny went down hard,
gun dropped from his hand,
his mother snatched it up
and sneered at us to go home.

and we ran.

that afternoon, Richard and i stood
in front of my house,
waiting for Johnny's father to arrive.
it didn't take long.

we didn't see Johnny
for three months.

lemons and oranges

in 4th grade
i walked to school every day.
down Helendale,
left on Hillrose,
right on Plainview.

every spring,
when lemons and oranges
filled the trees in our front yard,
my mom would pack a paper grocery bag
and instruct me to take the bag
to the crossing guard.

the bag weighed a thousand pounds
but i made sure every lemon and orange
made it safe,
not a one fell
from the bag.

i had a job
and i did it,
just as mother asked.

the crossing guard protected me
and my friends
from the big kids.
the bullies that would not hesitate
to beat the shit
out of 4th graders,
especially a big tall
kid with a giant head.

on the day i took
lemons and oranges
to the crossing guard,
the big kids,
the bullies,
quickly cornered me
and my friends, trying to
tear the bag away from me.

my mom always
told me not to fight,
she thought i
would hurt someone.
even in 4th grade.

turns out,

she was right.

kid in an iron lung

he had a rare disease
that kid across the street
the kid that didn't go to school
the kid that lived in an iron lung

my mom made me go see him
that kid
the weird kid
the one with the giant
black machine
in his dining room

his mom bought him everything
anything he wanted
we were all jealous
that kid
comic books and toys
and anything he wanted

he let me read
the comic books
and sometimes
i would steal them
stuff them in the back of my pants

my mom always caught me
we didn't have extra money for comic books
and i would have to march back across the street
apologize to that kid
the one with the iron lung
in his dining room

he didn't seem to mind much
he started to give them to me
so i wouldn't be considered a thief

as i got older i stopped going over
to see the kid across the street
and when i played stick ball or
street hockey with
Richard and Johnny
i didn't really care
if he looked out the window
sad because he had to live in an iron lung
because he couldn't play
stick ball or street hockey
or anything outside

several months after i moved away
he died
that kid across the street
the one with the iron lung
in the dining room

i wondered then if
he had looked out his window
watching Richard, Johnny and me
playing stick ball and street hockey

i wondered if he
hated me as much
as i hated myself
when i found out
he died

pretending grown up

Valerie lived across the street
from my house.
1971 or 2,
i can't really remember.
right around
the time of the big Sylmar quake.
1971, i guess.

she & i played as kids do,
back in the day, but
only when the other fellas weren't around.
Valerie had long dark brown hair,
brown eyes,
& i loved her.
openly.

at 7 or 8 years old -
too tall for my age, awkward, glasses -
Valerie tolerated me,
a trait that held true
for most women i would come to know.

i played dad & she played mom.
i'd come home late from work,
sit in my chair,
pretend to drink beer.
she did everything else;

even then the programming started.

sometimes we'd play dress up.
she'd put on pretend make-up

& i would watch her,
fascinated.
Valerie would
walk around,
pretending grown-up.
stylish & suave. i put on
pretend make-up too,
but her mom said
that's not allowed.

Valerie invited me
to her 8th or 9th birthday party.
i can't remember which one.
no other boys were allowed.
she called me her best girlfriend.

the last time we played house.
Valerie told me to be the mom.
she'd be the dad.
made sense at the time.

Valerie moved away,
i think. my memory's fuzzy
around certain events;
but i think of her, from time to time.
wondering if she is still playing house,

or if she found her way out.

a ballad for Robin Tucker

i fell in love with Robin Tucker early our 6th grade year
& i made the mistake of telling my best friend all about it -

Robin had bigger breasts than the other girls & a bigger heart.
kind, selfless, an absolute free spirit.
Robin got off the big yellow school bus one stop before mine,
at the trailer park, the true source of her scars.

other girls derided her for developing too fast.
boys would lay into her about the trailer park & an unfortunate rhyme
to her last name:

Robin Tucker, dirty fucker,
Robin Tucker, dirty fucker,

word got 'round that i loved Robin Tucker with every inch
of my prepubescent heart. the hazing immediate, rampant, absolute.

and i cried to my mother,
i didn't understand their derision, their antagonism, their rage.

after weeks of bullying i finally snapped, finally lost my mind,
finally welcomed my rage, finally turned to let them pick a fight,

meet us after 3:00 o'clock
you're dead shit, motherfucker
you should just walk away, pussy

my mother taught me to fight

don't wrap your hand around your thumb,
you might break it throwing a punch.

years earlier on the first day of 4th grade
the Navarro brothers befriended me.
i became part of the family, *la familia,*
and by the 6th grade the Navarro brothers
always stood at my side.

when the clock hit 3 a skinny white kid started
throwing punches, snot and spit flying.
three brown skinned boys stood ready to step in
and help, but that day i didn't need it.
that day everything changed.

no one talked to me for several months
& no one dare say a word about
Robin Tucker.

years later i bumped into Robin Tucker pushing a stroller
& walking next to a handsome man.

she looked at me, smiled, nodded, & kept moving down the street.

after a single heartbeat & a memory,
i turned & kept moving too –

a different version appeared in Raven Cage, 2019, issue 36

haircut

on a hot summer day
in 1973 my father dragged me
to the barbershop.
up Hillrose, around the corner,
next to a liquor store
and Jewish delicatessen.

i sat in a chair up next a giant
plate glass window,
bathed in the heat
of morning, the barber
and my father smoked
cigarettes, traded stores and
dropped ash indiscriminately.

a cluster of neighborhood punks,
up to no good and riding
Schwinn bicycles with baseball cards
clipped to the spokes,
stopped dead as they passed
the barbershop and the giant plate glass window.

they cracked jokes, pointed,
and made faces.
immediately scarred, i feared
sitting in the chair at the
barbershop.

five years later in 11th grade
i found myself in that chair
in the back of the shop,
getting my haircut to impress a girl.

more cackles, more ridicule.

the summer between 11th and 12th grade
i gained twenty pounds, grew two inches,
shaved my head and grew a beard.

first day of 12th grade the Vice Principal of Discipline
and Punishment stopped me as i walked on campus.

sir, your kids will be fine.

i stopped and turned.

how's that?

Mr. Yim looked, blinked, and said,

fuck, it's gonna be a long year

when he recognized me.

i ran my hand through my beard
and laughed.

down on the docks of Larsen's Boatyard

i remember Saturdays
going down
to Larsen's Boatyard
in Fish Harbor
w/my father.

he owned a 36-foot trimaran,
the *Loophole*,
& spent countless hours
working on it.

my father let me wander,
as long
as i stayed
on the docks,
or in the parking lot.
definitely
no further than the drydock.

i would pull trash
from the water,
chase little crabs
on jetty rocks,
buy cold cream sodas
in glass bottles
from the man
at the front office.

when the old trawlers
chugged by
i would wave,
& captains
& crewmen
would wave back.
seagulls would caw,
& lanyards would slap against
aluminum masts.

ripples from
the passing boats
changed the world.

despite my ability to swim
& love of the ocean,
i always feared falling off the docks
at Larsen's Boatyard.
i had heard of sea creatures
living beneath moored boats,
waiting for small boys to fall in.
but as long as my father kept watch
i knew i'd be okay.

and now i wonder,
48 years later,
who will watch over me,

when my father is gone?

Mrs. Samilian taught 8th grade math

every time Mrs. Samilian
slapped a dusty chalkboard
w/her pointer stick i smiled.

Mrs. Samilian taught 8th grade math.

some days she wore leather pants.
some days she slapped
the board w/ her pointer stick
while wearing leather pants,
and i would smile.

one day Mrs. Samilian called on me to
answer a problem at the board.

she wore leather pants,
slapped the board.

i could not stand up.

'is there a problem,
mr. jack?'
      slap

'you cannot come up
to the board?'
      slap slap

'why can you not
come up to the board,
mr. jack?'
      slap slap slap

finally, i stood.

girls cringed.
boys laughed.
one shouted,

'Jack's got a boner.'

and i did,
proudly.

Mrs. Samilian took one look,
smirked.

'you may go.'

instead of the principal's office
i went to the boy's restroom.
       slap, slap, slap.

when i explained to the principal,
he let it go. *he's just a boy.*
when i explained to my father,
he let it go, as well.

when i explained to my mother
she grounded me for two weeks
and made me apologize to Mrs. Samilian, who
politely declined when i tried to bring it

up.

a slightly altered version appeared in Horror Sleaze Trash, Summer 2020

typically, 13

At the age of 13 I was not an ideal child.

Hormones, anger, confusion: typically, 13. I don't know if there are options in labelling a 13-year-old – good, kind, bad, stupid, lazy – but the box next to each negative option would be checked for me.

Some days, when my father got home from work at or near dinnertime, he would greet my sister and I cheerfully. Even during the dark times, the depressive part of his bipolar condition, he would always say hello. He would inquire about school and life and things related, but my sister and I would merely grunt some minimal acknowledgement before returning our addictive gaze to the television.

Other days, my father didn't get home until after my sister and I were already in bed. We did not know why he came home late nor did we understand. We knew not to ask. My sister and I barely understood what my father did for a living, other the ubiquitous label of *salesman*. I don't really know now and I have been in one form or another of the sales profession for 25 plus years. Reading *Death of a Salesman* in 11th grade lit became the definition of sales and in my mind my father had become Willy Loman.

On those late nights he would tiptoe in, silent as the devil, creep up the stairs to his bedroom. The following morning, he might or might not appear at the breakfast table. Always a 50-50 deal.

Over time, my father's presence became more and more unpredictable. We never knew when he would be around or what mood he might be in or, ultimately, what to expect.

As time went by my sister and I learned how to act, when to be present, when to retreat. How to hide within ourselves or out bedrooms or out in the neighborhood with other kids.

My sister had her own challenges. Memory suggests that I was the good child and my sister the terror. But I know my sister's memory suggests the opposite. Most likely, she lived as the *vocal* terror and I lived as the *quiet* terror. It felt as if our father did not know how to manage our differing personalities. He retreated, just as we did.

Mother became the great arbitrator, stuck in between my father and the two of us. Sure, she made her choices and lived her life. But at what cost? I still don't know. Mom had to manage the daily bullshit my sister and I put her through; the ups and downs of two overly dramatic teenagers. Add it my father's shenanigans and you have a full plate.

In retrospect, I was shitty to both parents.

Until I had my own child and she went through her own temporary insanity as a teenager, I did not realize or acknowledge that I was very much part of the problem.

Around my 13th birthday my father went to the loony bin at St Joseph's Memorial Hospital in Orange, California. I know I am supposed to call it a Psych Ward, but a 13-year-old has a very singular vision of the world, especially in 1977. Empathy and/or sympathy were not high-ranking values I held in those days.

From 13 until 20/21 I had no sympathy for crazy: my family's, my own, or my father's. And I was unkind in thought and, often in action. What I know now could fill a hundred thumb drives and what I knew as a 13-year-old boy was practically nothing.

I wrapped myself in anger and held it as my mantra for the entirety of my teenaged years.

However, as time drifted by, I softened. Slowly having my father around became a highlight.

As my own career began to explode, time became precious and focus turned toward my own family.

During those years I went through a couple of shrinks. Not that they helped. It became an intellectual sparring session, one that I grew weary of, especially after paying $110 an hour.

The shrinks would explain away my father's behavior and that I had been a typical 13-year-old. The common refrain held that my father's illness was not my responsibility. Of course, I knew this, but accepting it held its own challenge.

At that age, to me, all fathers are drunks and crazy and spend time in the loony bin. That's the only way I could manage it as a teen and as a young adult. I know now that this thought is far from the truth, and yet, in those days, I wondered if a teen could make a perfectly normal father completely insane. I still wonder about that.

June 17, 1972

as a child i watched Watergate unfold / in glorious black & white.
each morning i sat at the breakfast table / with my father
reading every story with unbridled abandon.

i would ask my father / what it all meant / he would shrug / ask for the
sports page / drink another cup of coffee / smoke a cigarette.

i would ask my teacher / what it all meant / she would shrug / tell
me sit down / you're too young to understand /pass the quiz /
to those sitting behind you.

i would ask my principal / what it all meant / he would glare at me / tell
me i should / recite the pledge of allegiance / hold my hand / to my heart
/ & not tell Heather Jane Rottencrotch / to go fuck herself / when she
gossiped about / who liked who.

i asked President Nixon / what it all meant / in a letter / a year before /
he resigned / told him i understand right & wrong / how the rich would
always dominate the world / how people like me / would always be
powerless / how i lost faith / in the government.

at seven i knew what it all meant / 49 years later i still know / except
there are no more leaders / only demagogues & sheep

a slightly altered version appeared in Raven Cage, 2019, issue 36

i knew Kevin

i knew Kevin
a long time ago
summer between
9th grade & 10th
between junior high
& high school

Kevin & i pal'd around
mostly at school
a little around his house
but never at mine
i had too many secrets

Kevin seemed happy
content
looking forward
to high school
looking forward to
graduating
getting away
living somewhere else

i knew Kevin
right up to the day he blew his brains out with a shotgun

i spent the rest of that summer
trying to figure out
how he could pull
the trigger

i think we all did
those that knew Kevin

no one really talked about it
my parents didn't know
i never told them
& i didn't have
the courage to
talk to Kevin's parents

there was a funeral
reception
all the things
that go with death
but i wasn't invited
it probably didn't come up

when school started, we all forgot about Kevin
and i did too

except when i read about suicide
another kid dead
no rhyme or reason

i know why he did it
forty-something years later
we all have those moments
my finger has twitched on a loaded weapon

i still drive by his old house
another family owns it now
i wonder if they know the history
i wonder if anyone else remembers

or wonders when they drive by -

the day my father fought the Portuguese Navy

on a clear bright day in the mid-70s
my father fought the Portuguese Navy

out of the trimaran, the *Loophole*, racing across
an anchorage of large cargo vessels waiting
to dock and unload containers of plastic toys
and transistor radio sets, out past the breakers

high wind, high speed, skipping like a stone
across the wavetops

and then

nothing

wind dies, water becomes glass

the *Loophole* heads straight toward a Portuguese freighter filled
with cork and wine and Russian nesting dolls

the *Loophole* has a short keel, a tall mast
without wind there is nothing
but the current, momentum, and
the breeze from seagulls mongering for fish
to push her on

damn the torpedoes, full steam ahead!

we slam into the side of the freighter
  BAM!

and again
        BAM!

and again

crewman stare over the side, scream
qual é a sua porra problema?

i am shocked
my sister is shocked
my mother is shocked
and my father clinches his fist
screaming back at the Portuguese crew
profanities in multiple languages
fly back and forth

we bounce down the side of the freighter

BAM! BAM! BAM!

finally released to a wisp of wind
that takes us back to our mooring
in Fish Harbor
damaged but ultimately victorious

in our battle against the Portuguese Navy

busted

before i had a driver's license
my parents would drive me around.
depending on mood, time of day,
weather, and a variety of factors
my father would list.

i convinced my father to drive
me and my friends to LA Coliseum
for a concert.

he dropped us at the corner, gave
explicit instructions, when and where
to meet for the ride home.

at 15 i passed for 21 and in those days
no one really cared. i bought a fifth
of Jack Daniels and a pack of cigarettes
at a liquor store, before entering the concert.

we met up with a couple of girls from
Van Nuys, smoked cigarettes, ate hot dogs,
got sun burnt, and had the best time.

at 11 o'clock me and my friends stood
on a corner just outside the Coliseum,
waiting on my father.

we piled into the back of his company car.

when my mother asked my dad for
a cigarette he said,
ask your son.

i pulled out my pack of smokes, clearly
visible in a shirt pocket and handed them
to my mother. she coolly took
one, handed them back.

we'll talk about this later,
my father said.

i think i used the word *hypocrite* when we talked,
but i don't remember anything after,
other than
i knew i would always get caught
no matter how well i lied.

nursing home

when i was around
the age of 9 or 10
my grandmother
went into a nursing home.

several years later
she came out in a pine box,
destined for a cemetery
in Syracuse, NY.

i would go with my parents
and sister
to the nursing home,
to see my grandmother.

i would pop in,
say hello,
then get shoo'd out
by Filipino nurses.

my sister and i
wandered the halls,
zombies reaching out
to steal our youth.

every now and then we
would notice an empty bed.
no linen or blankets,
just a mattress.

'someone's dead,' i'd tell my sister.

yesterday we put my father
into a nursing home.
hospice care. six months,
probably less now that he's
locked down.

i'm indifferent in that moment.
i still walk the halls with
zombies, waiting for death,
waiting for my turn to
wonder where the hell i am
and when my turn will come

to be carried out in a pine box.

waking up in an alternative universe

The nurse tells me my father is sleeping and it may be best that I call at another time.

Trust me, I say. *He'll take the call.*

She transfers the call to a portable handset and walks it down the hall. I listen to the slap-slap of her shoes mark time with the thwack-thwack of my windshield wipers.

Hello, he says, his voice mud thick and a little confused.

Hello dad! Shouting because he is as deaf as i am.

Son! Thank God!

He snaps to life and pushes aside the grogginess of a midday nap. I picture him sliding into a sitting position on his small bed at the convalescent hospital. He is in hospice care now. Doctors tell me six months, maybe ten.

What's wrong?

This goddamned place is what's wrong.

He tells me in great detail about his day, about the convalescent hospital, about the crazies around him. His voice is strong and clear, his speech coherent. There is no dementia at the moment, no end-of-life fog. He tells me an off-color joke, one he has told me a hundred times, so often I have to force a laugh. He tells me about his roommate who has become his brother, tells me about the Irish nurse that shaves his face every three days.

When are you coming by?

I can't. For a while.

Why?

His voice flattens, deflates, filled with a sudden sadness, almost breaking.

The virus. No one from the outside can get into your hospital. Too dangerous.

The virus? I shake my head as I mention it. Life had become a bad sci-fi movie on one of the independent television stations, shown after midnight and hosted by a C level recovering alcoholic actor.

Bullshit is what it is...

I know, but thems the rules.

Long deep pause. Sometimes he would hang up the phone without another word or drop it to the floor. I wait before speaking and then here his rasp. Suddenly tired, resigned.

You know, I talked to your mother.

About?

My cancer. I'm not going out on the table.

Oh yeah?

Yeah. I'm gonna fight this. Not going out on the table.

The engine restarts and coughs back to life. I image him shuffling around the room without his walker or wheelchair.

That's all we really ever have. The will to fight.
He laughs.

I think I taught you that, son.

You did, dad. Absolutely.

He clicks off the phone without a *goodbye* or *talk soon* or *I love you.* Back to the norm, I think, as I smile to myself.

These days, days of Covid, all we have is the ability to fight and not enough of us do it. Maybe we should learn from an 81-year-old man with stage 4 cancer and a bad heart. Learn to fight. But nowadays we just hoard toilet paper and bottled water, huddle in our homes, and wait for death's knock.

addiction

addiction lays you bare
deep in your skull
dreams and life and love
disrupted
torn away, shattered,
empty glasses smashed against stone

it starts young, a gentle breeze,
smooth and slow, without conditions,
until you suddenly snap back to life,
screaming

you try to hide it,
the madness, insanity,
bipolar apparitions,
it will bury you in shame,
dark shadows, no breathing
but the art of deception
will always keep you whole

death dealers circle
on shiny jet thermals,
wait for the signature
full compliance
desecration of the soul

bury the humiliation in vaults made of concrete
outside the prison, the cage,
behind lock and key
you taste it, still wet on your fingers
wet copper or gun metal
sticks to your tongue

it's right here
in plain sight
but no one turns left at the signal
no one can see light fall from the stars

there are doctors and 12 steps
and hope for a future
but once it has caught you
the coils never forgive

there is pain in survival
when you dream of surrender
but if you can't face a mirror
how can you face the truth?

pills

red
or blue
red
or blue
red
or blue
red
or blue

one or two
five or six

2x daily
3x daily
not on an empty stomach
take with water
do not operate
a motor vehicle
or heavy machinery

side effects may include:
erectile dysfunction
sleeplessness
restlessness
diarrhea
over stimulation
sorrow and sadness
anger
acne
joint aches
weight gain / weight loss
tremors
headache
madness
blurred vision
high heart rate

heart attack
death

red
or blue
red
or blue

do not take with alcohol
do not take with opiates
do not take without supervision
do not take unless you want your
memory erased.
do not take unless you want to sit quietly,
staring out into space, lost in the fog
of your own memory

carbamazepine
topiramate
lamotrigine
risperidone
ariprazole
ziprasidone
clozapine

lithium

red
or blue
red
or blue
red
or blue
red
or blue.

two worlds

After my father got released from the psych ward at St. Joseph's Hospital all the beans spilled. As it turns out my father became more of a ghost to me, more so than I could have imagined. He truly lived in two worlds: one with his family and one where we did not exist.

And I understand that.

Every life is a multitude of "worlds." Out of necessity I certainly live in at least two words. One is the construct of poet/writer/editor/publisher. In other words, my creative world. But I have never blended my poet world with my family world. It would be like mixing caustic with acid. Explosive.

My father had two distinct worlds. In my mind, rather than family and non-family, I referred to them as sane and crazy.

Before the snap he lived in a world of alcohol and an undiagnosed bi-polar disorder. Some say the booze was to medicate the bi-polar. Some literature would suggest that, but I am no doctor and this statement is certainly open to conjecture. And I was not part of the conversation back then. Ultimately, I never understood my father's crazy. I saw it, lived with it, adjusted to it, but where that demon manifested from, I could not say. As an adult I learned about my father's troubled childhood, but is bi-polar environmental or genetic I couldn't say.

When my father found himself in the midst of a "normal" period of time, that is when the pendulum of bi-polar sat at the middle, neither up nor down, not manic nor depressive, I labelled him normal. Relatively normal. His normal.

*　*　*

Our neighborhood in the late 70s through the early 80s consisted of smokers, drinkers, working class. During the summer people would gather in backyards, watch baseball on portable black & white televisions, drink Coors beer from cans that had tear-tab openings, smoke Kent Cigarettes by the pack, drop racial epithets without concern, and live a relatively simple life. The children of these parents played baseball all day, swam in the community pool, played smear the *queer* in the big field, beat the shit out of each other at the smallest provocation, stole candy, cigarettes and Playboy Magazine from the 7Eleven from across the street, and rode skateboards to the local mall. We cursed, lied, fucked, and tried to *"pretend grown-up"* every waking hour.

But from behind the doors of quiet homes in a small tightknit community cracks appeared. Crazy came and went, and sometimes stayed.

My sister and I didn't know any other world. We only had the one in which we lived, as children. You can pick your nose but you can't pick your parents.

It came as no surprise that my father became an alcoholic. To what extent I didn't knew, and to this day I don't know the full impact of his disease. The older I grew the farther I flew. Age was my excuse to grow distant from my family, especially my father. It's a bullshit excuse but really all I have.

What I didn't expect to hear about was my father's infidelity. That came as a shock.

But it shouldn't have.

My father had always been a looker and a charmer. All the women in my life have been charmed by my father. Even in his old age, within weeks of turning 81, my father used charm as easily as breathing.

I saw it all the time. My earliest memories have moments when my father would flatter a waitress or sandwich maker, or any female with whom he would interact. And then, I suppose, he went a step too far, a step I know as well.

Booze and mental illness make a person do stupid things. It's easy to say, *oh he's a drunk, he can't help himself.* Or, he's bi-polar, *his condition makes him do that.* Shrinks have told me I am free of any mental illness, but I've been a drunk. I know that world and everything I did while drunk is on me. No one else. In my mind I could quit, why couldn't anyone else? Why couldn't my father?

I quickly learned that the values I placed on myself were not necessarily applicable to others. Alcoholism is a disease. I still struggle with that concept.

The world my father lived in must have held many challenges. Living with an undiagnosed mental illness and alcoholism is living a nightmare. Just from observation I can testify to that. But when the mind becomes scrambled you never know what will come out.

When my father snapped, I was 13. I discovered his different lives, different worlds, and I discovered mental illness had a name: bi-polar. It would prove to be one of the many new words I would associate with my father.

out to kill rabbits

the first day we dressed out in
high school gym a senior
boy punched me in the face,
called me queer, as a choir
of boys howled in derision.

a rabbit sits atop a grassy
knoll, eats grass and watches
for danger.

at 16 i had yet to accept
my awkwardness,
long legs and gangly arms;
acne, sadness, and general ineptitude.

a rabbit hides during daylight, in
thick bushes or down holes
in the earth, fearful of predators
and potential death.

throughout 10th grade everyone
picked on me, put me in a corner,
bullied me into complete sorrow.
but i learned to fight, learned to
shout them down, learned to
run, learned to keep my secrets
locked down tight.

coyotes and wolves and kids
with rocks stalk the rabbit, but
if the rabbit is smart, they
stay safe. they must always
be smarter that those that wish them harm.

senior year i reached full height, full strength.
mind quick and nimble and more clever
than bullies. i outgrew the noise
of high school, but not before
breaking bones and crushing souls.

> *a rabbit cornered can be a fearsome thing*
> *and they will fight for survival when*
> *running away is no longer an option.*

just after winter break, senior year,
i found myself in front of the damning
gaze of a vice-principal, his face red,
voice rough from yelling. i had become
the bully.

> *a rabbit's life is short due to so many*
> *predators. life in the wild is*
> *always a struggle.*

upon graduation i left high school,
never looked back. i still break bones
of predators,

out to kill rabbits.

into the abyss

we are all orphans
now
lost in the desert
alone in a crowd
clichés all
but still
buried in deafening truth -

we used to walk
together
in times of conflict and chaos
in times of celebration and survival
but those days
i fear
are gone
those days
but a memory

we are split
divided
a thousand tribes
balancing on a thin
wooden beam
a beam that crosses
a chasm between yesterday
and tomorrow

we struggle with balance
maybe the beam will widen
into two or four or
enough for us
all to cross

without falling deep
into the abyss

gaining on us

they say once a snowball
gains a certain amount
of downhill momentum
you cannot stop it.

hypothetically, the snowball will consume anything
in its path;
trees, homes, people, lives,
the snowball will only stop
when it collides with forces bigger,
stronger, more durable than
the force a snowball
brings.

my father continues to build momentum.

my sister and mother called,
said, *it's too much.*
they said, *you need to do something,*
as if i have any skillset to manage crazy.

i talked to my father this weekend.
he seemed coherent. and yet
he spoke about flying gliders, as a boy,
in upstate New York, as if it was yesterday,

when the snowball hits and rumbles
to a stop, there is devastation,
there is death, there is pain,

once, as a child, i flew in a glider,
with my mother. i sat on her lap.

my job was to pull the knob that released
the glider from the tow plane.
i did it well.

we soared above Wisconsin, and dairy farms
and green hills. we soared above the noise of
a crazy world, free within the clouds, heavy on
the wind;

how i wish i was in a glider now, high above
it all,

but i am here on a mountain, standing before
a snowball, trying to stop something

that is inevitable.

my father's eyes

my father has beautiful blue eyes,
eyes we share.
when i look into his eyes i see myself,
my mortality.
i see fire and fight, a longing to
understand why we've locked
him away at the loony bin.

some days they are remarkable and clear.
a mischievous glimmer,
still a boy raising hell, pulling pranks,
all with a golden heart.

some days his eyes are gray. he cannot
speak well enough to make you understand
and frustration builds.

and through it all he still helps those
around him. Russell, the retired Marine,
wonders that halls; Bill is so medicated
he can barely stay awake;
Randy, with Tourette's, calms down when
my father looks him in the eye.

so much frustration in fading, when the mind
snaps and a body slows, we hang on
and fight for each moment, each breath.
every day a new hope and a new disappointment.

we all dance in front of a mirror
and only stop when they take
the mirror away,

and blue eyes slowly close.

slowly dying

i used to laugh
at the "i've fallen & i can't get up"
commercials.

not anymore.

my father called me,
expressed joy that my daughter
had made Dean's List at university.
he was coherent.
i understood every word.
the fog had lifted.

for a moment.

i heard shuffling,
things falling in the background.
he muttered, *i'm okay,*
but i knew.

my mother answered her phone
on the third ring.

you know where dad is, right?

no.

she found him in the backroom.
on the floor.
crumpled old linen waiting on the wash.

i have to call EMT to get him up.

i called my sister instead.

everything's fine.

last night, while my mother ran
to get dinner, he found a door he could open.
and disappeared into the night.

the Sun City police department found him,
wandering the alley. no cane, no walker, no wheelchair.

he said,
i just want a carton of cigarettes.

he is dying, cancer returned, outlook grim,
prepare yourself.

i say give him the smokes and a liter of bourbon.
go out kicking and screaming, not lost
in a fog, fading faster than the dimming sun

in winter's sky.

escape the loony bin

he pulled his catheter out
and ran free in the streets
one last time before finally
slowing to a stop.

he sat down in the middle
of a crosswalk on a busy street,
exhausted.

traffic did not move, no one
knew what to do with a crazy
half-dressed man who blocked
their way, blocked their lives
and their misery, their transport
from one sin to the next.

he just laughed as they called out
to him, pleading to move.

as cars rattled close nothing
could pull that smile from his lips,
even as nothing could quill the roar in
his skull, all the words he wanted
to say, yet nothing every came out
clear enough to be understood.

he just sat there until the cops
called, said,
your father is blocking traffic,

and i thought,
good —

cosmonauts sing old David Bowie songs

it's cold here,
on the surface of the moon,
but i can dance
without effort
and my knees
no longer ache.

on earth,
under the Phoenix sun,
my father
reads old magazines.
he pines for
communion
with family,
his wife,
his daughter.
me.

he sits in a
small room,
dimly lit
with a low
wattage bulb,
waiting.

COVID hit,
down the hall,
two dead.

Randy still screams *help*
and Henry dozes
in his wheelchair.

young mothers

abandon nursing jobs,
abandon old people
in dimly lit rooms,
sitting alone,
waiting.

and i bounce
from crater to crater,
waiting
for the operator.
she won't pick up.
no one's home.

lurking

my father never slept normal hours
which proved tricky
some days

it could be 3 am,
my father sitting at the kitchen table
smoking a cigarette, drinking coffee
where you been?
out, doing nothing
i never knew if he just woke up
or never went to sleep

it could be 12 noon,
my father asleep on the couch
television blaring
images of the Challenger exploding
on a continuous loop

it could be 1 am
sitting on the couch
girlfriend practicing new skills
a shuffling upstairs
a creaking on the steps
a light in the kitchen snapping on
what are you doing?
nothing, please don't come in

even in death
my father didn't do normal,
he just closed his eyes
and went away
forever.

bi-polar mind and a commission paycheck

latch-key kid
growing up
both parents
working 9-5
rich kids up
in Anaheim Hills
call you poor
they call anyone
different
poor

mom works
to make ends meet
father did what he could
bi-polar mind and a commission paycheck

you could tell
the day of the month
based on what you ate
things got thin
at the end of the month

out on the road
chasing the deal
late nights
and overnighters

sometimes we'd celebrate
meet him at LAX or SNA
i'd carry his suitcase
dream of the day
when i hit the road

my father and i trade
stories
warriors of the road
hustle the customer
hustle the deal

we have that in common

now he waits on death
sitting in his overstuffed chair
faded Navy baseball cap propped on
his balding head
trading stories
memories

i still have miles to go
he measures moments in inches
there are fewer stories to tell
but the hustle is still there

blue skies over the Pacific

i am bored
bored and tired
and writing the same old thing
once again.

bored and tired
but still drawing a breath
each morning when
i wake.

and today it did not rain,
in California.
it did not snow
in the mountains,
there were no flash floods
in the desert.

but how many died today?
how many more diagnosed?
how many alone, hiding behind
locked doors, trembling in fear,
paranoia.

how many birds took flight,
scattered amongst tall buildings
and high trees?
how many children laughed
because that is what children do?
how many lovers found joy
beneath tattered sheets?

how many stars shine
above a trembling earth?
i check my friends,
each morning.
they are there, out in the world.
they are there, with fearsome fight
and a will to keep moving.

i am alone in my bunker.
too many wires connecting
to a dissonant world,
to friends and neighbors
and people i barely know, but
we understand the fight,
we understand dreams and hope
and blue skies over the Pacific.

part one: ...of light

my mind buzzes,
a constant refrain;
i hide in shadows
wrapped tight
with the absence of light.

i cannot move,
i cannot see or hear or drive
over the speed limit without veering
into
oncoming traffic.

it is monday,
now sunday;
days hold no meaning.
pardon my manners,
where was i?

fragments litter across
my eyelids;
here, now;
then & there;

five more minutes,
i promise i will get up.

home at noon, sleep until three;
back to work. sorry, i'm late;
i had an appointment.

a single bullet
sits in the chamber;
everything black;
absence of light
absence of life

who are you? i can't remember?
do i know you?

this thing, this life,
holds no value;
i hold no value;

these pills;
this bottle,
now empty...

wrapped tight
with the absence of light;

everything's black;

everything –

part two: ...of life

maybe it's time to throw out
the tv,
computer,
& subscription to the
ny times -

maybe it's time to stand upright,
walk amongst the other
bipeds,
the emus & orangutans -

maybe i should adjust the light,
note the absence of life, delve
deep into the subtext of this
gloryhole mediocrity -

maybe i should slow down,
stop running, live a quiet life
in the desert, out in the sand &
yuccas & Joshua trees -

maybe i should pull the needle from
my arm, the rolled dollar from my nose -

maybe i should forget everything & simply
learn how to exist -

330 miles

i will sit behind the wheel, lost in thought,
and drive east 330 miles to phoenix.

i will walk up the steps
of a worn-out nursing home.

i will talk to my father, try to understand the words
his addled brain lets out.

i will try to keep a brave face.
i am the oldest child. it is my job.
keep 'the brave face.'
my mother will busy herself
because that is what she has always done.

i will try to smile, tell funny stories, keep the mood light.

i will walk out of his room and lose it
in a hallway or just outside a front door,
or as i drive to a dealer, or just after i score, but i will lose it.
completely.

i will spend the night
in the guest room of my parents' house
but not sleep, even for a moment.

i will say goodbye to my father
before i drive 330 miles west, back to work,
and a life that feels less important.

i will park my car, go inside, make
a meal or drink a beer, and watch television.

i will put my phone on a table and wait
for the inevitable.

yesterday
my dad told me he had cancer,
again.
he's been down the road twice
but this time

it's serious.

VA doc suggests we ask
for a second opinion
outside the system.
my father loves the VA
but i am not so sure.
the onion peels only so far
without help.

over the years
i have lost faith
in the *system*.

it's cheaper to bury a vet than care for a vet,
vets like to tell me.
you're dying from birth.
maybe that's true.

at 55 i've done some living but at 80
my dad has seen more
than I can imagine.

my dad won't live forever
maybe not another year.

no one really dies
except the forgotten.

and that's all this poem really is about,
an attempt to not be forgotten,

because that's all i've got left.

i'm not a big believer in heaven or hell
but i've witnessed both
in the eyes of my father,
the eyes of strangers,
my own mirror late at night.

in a few days
i will sit with my dad,
trade stories,
memories.

some will become poems.

he will not be forgotten
and neither will i.
he's in my words.

that's all i've ever really had -

where did we park the car?

they stand on corners near my office,
a place i go to find silence,
now that work has dried up.

they stand on the corners,
near my office, selling masks
that mothers and grandmothers,
- *madres y abuelas* -
make on old sewing machines.
mass production in a living room.

there's no work to be found in
the Home Depot parking lot.
there are no houses to clean.
everyone has a hustle to survive,
regardless of color.

the masks are good. strong.
i bought two. ten dollars each.

i feel the guilt of survival,
the guilt of having enough to make it,
the guilt of having supplies well before
the storm settled over my town.

nothing feels real anymore.
nothing is the same.

when the lights come up
and the movie comes to an end,
we will walk into the brightest light
and try to remember

where did we park the car?

sometimes a moment is all we need

around the age of three
my daughter spied a man
sitting on a bench
in a food court.
he appeared tired & sad,
alone.

my daughter said,
he needs a hug.

he looked up at me,
his eyes weary, filled w/sorrow,
& grief;
his eyes heavy, full of defeat
as if to say *what do i do?*

i just smile & nod
it's okay.

the man on the bench
opens his arms & my daughter
hugs him.
sweet, innocent, no further question
or concern.

my daughter skips away,
smile wide across her face.
for a moment the world feels normal,
filled w/ the innocence of
a three-year-old girl.

'i'm dying, right?'

i called my father today.

he mumbles his words,
when they finally show up,
and can barely hear my response.

there's a lot of screaming
and repeating,
on my part.

he says 'huh' and 'what'

i am not sure
where that patience
comes from. it
didn't come
from him.
it didn't come
from my mother,
sister, aunts, uncles,
cousins.

patience is not a virtue
around my Thanksgiving table.

he asks when
i'm coming out,
am i calling from
the lobby, am
i helping him
escape the
End Days Convalescent Hospital

i remind him
about COVID19,
and New York City,
and how i'm fine
but my friends are
struggling.

he says the food is
shit and wants to
go home, but then says

i'm dying, right?

i say, *we all dying,
just at different speeds.*

he laughs.
i tell him this
every time i call.

for the moment
he knows who i am,
where i live, what i do,
but the armor has become
tarnished and battle lines
not as clear.

soon echoes will
be memories and
Saturday night
just another day.

Riverdale Avenue

Living in a house of mental illness is a trip.

Over the course of my first 13 years of life on this big blue planet I had no clear understanding. People are crazy and they just are, there's no reason, at least in my mind. You're born that way.

In 1977 mental illness existed, but not as a part of polite conversation in my white working-class Presbyterian neighborhood where tolerance for "things" outside the norm was not acceptable. And by "norm" I am suggesting the neighborhood's definition, and no one else. By modern standards my neighborhood would be considered racist, bigoted and hugely xenophobic. *If it ain't white, it ain't right,* could have flown as a flag right next to the old Stars and Stripes. That is, of course, if anyone dared speak up.

At some point in 1977 my father snapped. Since early adulthood my father had lived with undiagnosed bi-polar disorder. At least in my understanding. Alcohol managed the highs and time managed the lows. And the lows could stretch out across weeks and months.

My sister and I were well aware of my father's ups and downs. We could get away with just about anything if we played it right. At an early age we both knew how to exploit an opportunity.

One sunny day my father announced that he was going to purchase a TRS-80, affectionately known as a Trash 80 in upper Nerdsville. My sister and I had no clear idea about what computers could do. But we found out.

Over the remainder of that summer, she and I fought for computer time. My sister, who was five years younger than me, eventually lost interest and I became manic in my pursuit of understanding a computer, spending endless hours writing BASIC code, which made the computer "work." Tiny stick figures would walk across the screen, my name flashing and exploding, balloons floating from the bottom of the screen to the top. I thought myself a programmer.

But I lost interest as well and moved to other preoccupations.

At $600 dollars our Trash 80 did not come cheap. Six hundred dollars in 1977 is roughly $2,500 in 2020.

Mental illness is a trip.

It was not always high times when my sister and I could get things we wanted but never really needed.

Every time my father went on a downward spiral it ended up a scary time for the family. He would come home from work and immediately nap on the couch. He lost interest in the small things and it felt like he just disappeared altogether.

Down days were scary dangerous times. Sudden mood shifts. Nights when he didn't come home until well past my bedtime.

The day my father snapped and ended up in a psych ward changed me forever. I lost any ability to communicate with my father. An invisible barrier went up and stayed in place until his cancer returned.

I am told my father did not recognize me when I went to the hospital with my mother for a visit. It's not something the family readily talks about, and why would you? I know there was therapy and recovery and all things great and small associated with mental illness. And I don't remember any of it.

Memory does remind me about meds, the correct dosage, doctors' appointments, job loss, new jobs, but they are fragments. My mother shielded me from much of it, of that I am sure, and my father did not talk about it. Not that I asked. In those days you just talk about anything, out of the "norm." And you didn't talk to your father, unless you were trying to explain away punishment.

On occasion my mother would explain about my father's past, how he grew up living with grandparents after his father's divorce, how his life wasn't stable in those very early years. Without a stable role model whose behavior toward family could be learned, his destiny was one of challenge. Combined with alcoholism and bi-polar disorder, my father kept his emotions locked deep.

As I grew older, I knew what battles my father faced. Over the course of his life mental illness has never been more than inch away from his life, and mine. Once you are born into a house of mental illness you live there forever.

the very definition of sorrow

my father sits
in a room
waiting.

waiting for
a son to call,
or a daughter
or wife.

every time i
call the loony bin,
one of the inmates
picks up
the phone
and
listens to
my pleas
to talk to my father.
to just say hello.
to just check in,
before the voice says
no.

when COVID
hit his convalescent
hospital,
where he sits
waiting to die,
a place where
the outside
is not supposed
to get inside,

the lunatics
have taken
over the asylum,
and young nurses
with small
children
no longer come to work.

i sit on hold,
waiting (again)
to talk to my father,
talk to somebody sane,
somebody that might
know something
about anything.

but no one knows
anything.
when it gets bad
no one seems to care.

i sit
and i wait
as anger
creeps into
every
fucking
cell
of
my body.

the thought
of my father
dying alone

in that room
without
family
at his side
is the very
definition
of sorrow.

tomorrow
i will get in
my car,
drive 330 miles
east,
and kick down
the door
of my father's
convalescent
hospital…

but i won't.
he told me not to come.
he told me to stay safe.

and to break him out when all of this is over.

zombie

my mind drifts
& i wonder if
Covid has taken over,
like a zombie movie,
everyone
infected –

maybe my father
is a zombie –

he'd like that.
he could express his
rage
& fuck people
up -

grace has fallen away

my sister calls.
she sounds tired.

she
is
tired.

she waits until
i find my moment of calm
before she speaks.

two people have it.

i don't have to ask
what she means.
this is a conversation
thousands of people have every day,
nowadays.
these days.

Covid days.

you don't have to ask.

my father is in a nursing home.
330 miles east in Sun City, Arizona,
locked down.
memory unit.

two people, his wing.

his hall. they just started testing. everyone.

the dystopian amerikan gov't
hijacked PPE - masks,
gowns, face shields – Homeland
takes control of all shipments,
because: China, the new evil empire.

an outbreak felt
inevitable.

death creeps down
a hallway in the
memory unit.

he's been through
cancer three times.
he's down to 139 lbs.
he is old.

if *Covid* takes my old man,
some might say,
it is what it is and there's no one to blame,
but i know who to blame.

over the past 45 years i've fallen away
from god and religion but my father never did.
even in the shallows of his own madness
he maintained a conversation.

i don't sleep much, so i talk to god.
real or not, it doesn't hurt,
especially when grace has fallen away
from the scattered tribes who
live near the tides of turbulent seas.

splendor of normalcy

we live in a time of
choking madness
a late-night Japanese
monster movie w/o sub titles
a burnt-out rain forest in
New South Wales,
Australia

we are mired in the largess
of our own nightmares
as we dare not to dream
lest these dreams come true

we struggle here,
those of us at the bottom
life drifts from pay check
to pay check, while the rich
live on magnificent yachts
as they wait out a storm
encroaching upon a long
horizon

we hide behind doors, behind windows,
wait for promises fulfilled, hope
within grasp, a chance to return
to the splendor of normalcy
and yet we fall short of
hopes and dreams, simple moments
needed to survive.
moments of warmth
and kindness
and sanity

when we look toward
heaven we long for the
freedom to have a heaven,
to speak of a heaven,
we long for the grace of
humanity, we long for the
peace of serenity;
but we're not there now,
we are further away
with
each
rasping
breath,
and now

today

we no longer care for each other,
we no longer know each other,
we no longer lift our hands
and help each other,

this is just a poem,
these are just words,
this is just a passing ship,
bells cry
in the night,
yet we are not
at an end, not yet,
our paths remain
shared, our future
remains
optimistic

my mother is in a hospital
and my father lays dying
friends and family
are buried on Hart Island,
a lunatic roams the long hall
of American legacy

we are out of work
we face oblivion
we stand together well
within the grasp
of quiescence
but we will rise up,
we will stand up,
we will finally find a way
to capture light within
the palms of our hands
and
we will, once again, remember
how to breathe -

last dance

My father is rapidly approaching that last dance of life. Musicians are in place, songs selected, my mother's best dress is at the dry cleaners; we stand at the ready for the last rasping breath.

And when he goes, we will gather. Family and friends will remember a life well lived. It will not be of mourning but of celebration. At least, in that moment.

We will forget the horror, the tears, the final madness that ate away at my father's existence. In death there is life there is truth with each step we take away from the last goodbye.

Over the last few years my father disappeared. The man I grew to know, to begrudgingly respect, to turn to for advice, to trade stories and dirty jokes died years before his death.

And in those remaining years there were true moments of clarity, when his blue eyes sparkled, when his laughter was genuine and not fraught with fear. Moments that occurred with less frequency as time dragged on. He would slip back beneath the waves, deep into a well of faraway days.

I am not sad. I said goodbye to my father before the madness, Alzheimer's, Dementia. Before he gave up, before the stories became delusion, before his words became insane. I have always loved my father, as a son, a friend, a caretaker, a colleague, a provider. That love will always remain. His dark shadows that came around when the meds failed, when the booze regained control, when the bipolarity became a parlor game, have already started to fade.

A last note remains, one that will carry through the coming days and nights, and it is a sound as light as a feather drifting away.

a special kind of cruelty

the convalescent hospital
where my father
whittles away time as he
awaits a preordained end
started a new visitor policy.
just like prison.
the internees are on one side
of the glass,
friends and family and hospice
workers
on the other side.

i received a picture from
my brother-in-law. mom and
sister on one side,
my father on the other,
talking on cell phones.

seems like a special kind of cruelty
for both sides of the coin.

i haven't talked to my father
in a few weeks now, maybe it's
been a month. not sure why.
shadows and memories
hold me in place.

> *i have a plant in my garage, set*
> *before a window.*
> *diffused light allows*
> *new growth to this plant.*
> *direct sunlight almost killed it.*

an ordinary tragedy

three old ladies
sit together and watch
as their husbands
fall apart.

in the lunch room
three old men sit in
wheelchairs slowly
drifting toward
oblivion, each with
a different path,
each at a different
stage.

three old ladies watch
their men fade,
they have their own paths
as well.

they chatter a bit,
a sort of normalcy settles,
until a patient
throws a train to
the floor.
another yells *fuck* repeatedly
until others
yell at him to just
shut the fuck up.

the old ladies barely notice
there's no reason to be startled.
it's an ordinary tragedy.

Alzheimer's, Parkinson's,
Dementia, Tourette's.
all the demons are here.

my father observes
without comment.
Bill falls asleep.
another man wanders off
in his wheel chair.

three old ladies care for their men,
tend to their needs,
and try to stay calm.

these days

i don't sleep much
these days.

yeah, there's a lot going on
&, yeah, i struggle with time management
&, yeah, we all need to do what we do
to make ends meet,

but i don't sleep much
these days.

i'm learning about new things.
dementia.
micro-strokes.
Parkinson's.
hospice care.

i've been to the bin,
met the loons.
it's disheartening to wait for death.

i should take my father home.
i should be able to manage his illness.
i should be able to deal with his insanity.
i should understand mental illness.
but i can't.

yeah, i don't sleep much
these days.

he's a threat,
they say.
to himself, your mother, and anyone around him,
they say.

at 130 pounds
he's not a threat
to anyone,
but there are rules
and regulations to follow.
in polite society.
in life.
in Phoenix, Arizona.

the only freedom left is the grave

and soon,
i will make a drive across a desert,
dressed in
black coat,
black pants,
black soul,

and put him in the ground.

sounds a lot like jesus

drunk in a motel room
in Blythe, California.
not a pretty picture.

shadows across the sky, a canvas,
deep blue, purple and black.
even Van Gogh held onto
mystery w/every stroke of
his brush.

and like Van Gogh i have demons,
we all have demons.
some are long term visitors and
some just come and go.

at 56 i don't have a great many
steps yet to take, not a lot of places
left to go. life has treated me
better than most
and my demons have
held their distance until now.
until today. until i looked in the
mirror and saw the same blue
eyes of my father.

he's 81 and dying, lying in wait in
a convalescent hospital in
Phoenix, Arizona. they took out
all the clocks because the
ticking notes the passage of time.

i'm not prepared for the next 25 years,
i'm not prepared for tomorrow,
but my demon has a first name
that sounds a lot like jesus, and, i think,
he and i will work out just fine.

sometimes violence is the norm

my father
is crazy.
without question.
my mother is
crazy too.
she puts up
with his
insanity.
enables it.
motivates it.
my mother
is a great woman
and i love her
without question,
but sometimes
parents
are a burden
i do not
want.

parents grow old,
develop Dementia, Parkinson's,
a thousand ailments large
and small.

and we cannot
say what we want
to say.
the children
of the insane
must
remain silent.

but we hang in.
we suffer.

they don't mean it,
some say
they don't know
what they are saying,
some say
it's your job now,
some say

every day
i watch as they diminish,
as crazy takes
greater hold,
as the devil
stares back at
me when i
seek a clear
moment

you try to be
the better person,
you try to live up
to societal expectations,
you try to be
the loving son,
but it's hard

my father is
not my father
he is something different
he has changed
he is not really human

he has become his disease

       have patience
they say
       his time is coming near
they say
       they took care of you now it's your turn to take care of them
they say

and i simmer
as anger grows
as torment
tears my soul into
tiny pieces

my hands
ball into fists
as i pick a fight
with the biggest
biker in the bar,
hoping the pain
of my beating
will somehow
make me feel
real again –

sinking the titanic

Fish Harbor felt like magic
overnight on the boat
end of the dock
water flat and glassy
halyards clanking against masts and booms
a slight breeze barely touches the sea

you wave to fishing trawler captains
watch first light climb the eastern sky
another day begins

December 7th, mid 70s
i can't remember the year
a US Navy barge rips my father's boat
a trimaran named *Loophole* from her mooring
tears her to shreds
there will be no recovery
no 'raise the *Titanic*'

no more Saturdays at the docks
no more trips across the channel to Catalina
no more battles with the Portuguese Navy

it took years to realize
the death of the *Loophole*
allowed a move from meth infested Tujunga
to yuppie-controlled Orange County

one drug to another
financed by the death of a dream

crushed

i love driving across
the Mojave Desert.
long wistful stretches of
asphalt; due east to Phoenix,
due west to Los Angeles.

most days it is incredible,
w/the radio off, windows
down, thoughts ping pong
in your skull, as a sun climbs or falls,
as the moon follows your path,
as wind whips through mesquite
and creosote.

i never notice time, just traffic,
just landmarks, just rest stops,
where i park and write poems
in a tattered composition book.

today, i noticed time, every second.
my mind clutters w/thoughts
of my father and his internment
at the loony bin; the shame
and guilt i feel leaving him there.

what do you want, i ask.
get me out of here, he pleads.

he is combative and crazy
w/stage 4 cancer, a problem
w/his heart, a risk of aneurysm.
at 81 he has lived a life full and true,
and now?

he cries when i leave, i cry when
i get to my car. after 100 miles i pull off
the highway, head deep into the desert
and scream at god.

nothing but shame,
grief, and sadness.

and now…

now that i am home,
in my bed, my mind focuses
on the week, on the job,
on chores, on life,
i can only think i failed
my father.

it's a son's job to take care
of a parent just as a parent
once took care of a son.

on my fingers i count
his remaining months.
hope for more, pray for the best,
but the endgame is clear, and when
he's gone all i will have is

ash and sorrow.

all ghosts are waiting

1.

when my ex died unexpectedly,
alone in an apartment she
could not afford,
in a city where conformity
ruled & no one dared stray
from the dotted line;
in her state of financial ruin
brought on by a cancer she
blamed on me;
i thought that day, that moment
i would return to sanity;

but i was wrong -

2.

her ghost haunts me,
still & i know i should let it
go, but this ghost is real;

she follows me around,
let's me know she is watching;
i have grown used to it -

3.

her ashes sit on a shelf of
tchotchkes, at the top
next to smaller cedar boxes of dead dogs;

her box is colorful, secured by
a small diary lock, the kind
you could crush with your fingertips;

she left no instructions on a proper
burial and my daughter didn't know
what to do, so she sits on a top shelf;

watching -

4.

it's cold
at the top of Mount Baldy;
a few people gather
in clusters of twos and threes;
i came with my ghost
and a backpack holding
a gray paper box
filled with ashes;

i started at 4am,
made good time,
hit the summit in 5 hours,
a record, for me;

at the far edge of the rounded
peak i reach into
my backpack and pull out
the gray paper box,
set it down on behind a large
stone, used as a wind break;

the sun slowly arches across
a bright, blue sky; it is a perfect
day; i remove the lid, pull out
a bag of gray ash;
it is heavy, nearly three pounds,
all that remains;

i kept tablespoon of ash, put it in
a beautiful crystal jar, placed it back on
the shelf, for my daughter, for the
day she wants to remember;

but on the mountain i let it fly,
emptied the bag into the wind,
a temporary cloud rising and
falling on the breath of god;

a ranger approached, but i caught
him in the corner of my eye;
i had a permit, she would have liked
that, being prepared for a change –

5.

death is all around me.
present, past, future.

i am waiting.
i can hear footsteps approach.

all the ghosts are waiting.
more ghosts than living.

there are footsteps
approaching.

one more ride

there's a nice breeze
blowing in from the ocean.
it moves up and over
the Santa Ana Mountains,
across my back porch.
it cools the thick wet heat
of the desert.

there's a long stretch
of black asphalt that
passes near my shelter.
some nights i walk
out to the edge of
that road and set my feet
atop the line
where asphalt touches dust.

i imagine breaking
my father free of his hiding,
there in Sun City, behind
the virtual bars of
convalescence, of hospice.

one last ride down
a long stretch of black asphalt.

one summer just after receiving
my license from the California
Department of Motor Vehicles
my father and i drove from
Syracuse, New York to
Orange, California.

my sister and mother stayed
behind and would eventually fly home.

just outside of Springfield, IL
my father handed me the keys
to his company car and pointed
west, said just keep driving
until you are no longer in the mood.

Springfield to Denver is 910 miles.
all flat. all straight highway.
the old man's sedan could hit 100mph
no problem, and the moment he
fell asleep it did.

every now and then he would blink awake
and i would ease back some.
he'd ask, you okay? i'd say, sure.
he'd drift off and i would hit the pedal.

we ate thick top sirloin steaks at a roadside joint
somewhere in Kansas, deep in the shadow
of the Rocky Mountains.

when i touch that highway, the line between
asphalt and dust, i long for one more run,
one more ride,

driving with crazy.

elegy for my father

this is not the time for sorrow or sadness,
this is not the time
for regret.

life moves forward,
with debilitating slowness,
and maddening sobriety
as we hold tight the rails
when seas begin
to rise.

there is magic in life
and
in death.

now my father captains his ship toward Heaven's forever,
held tight in eternities bliss,
his smile bright and strong,
his laugh loud and unending.

there is no pain, no sorrow,
no cancer,

no madness

only the unending joy as he watches
us travel the earth,
trying to endure,
awaiting a time
when we all meet

again.

time never stops for the dead

we sit around a kitchen table
at my sister's house
Peoria, AZ.
waiting it out.

my father's memorial,
days away,
nothing left to do
but sit and scrape through
old memories.

boxes of old pictures
litter a kitchen table.
is that you?
and
oh, look at this one?
and
everyone looks is so different.

we review plans.
change plans.
buy urns.
create agendas.

but there is nothing
important left to do.

outside a bright Arizona sun
continues to melt asphalt.
black birds hide in low bushes.
police sirens echo from
a main street.
gray clouds tease from
a distant horizon.

maybe we should order pizza?
where is the whiskey?
what time is it?

what are we doing?

my niece mixes strong
drinks and we toast
my father
grandpa
the old man

we remember
without speaking
but the present
keeps knocking

just as there is
no rest for the
wicked, time never
stops

for the dead.

and so, the story ends

On June 4, 2020, my father passed away quietly in his sleep.

That morning he woke, dressed, had breakfast, talked to a nurse, and went to sleep forever.

As with many father/son relationships there are a thousand questions that remain and will go unanswered. But I don't feel any regret. Perhaps I should, but the last few years have been lost to dementia. The moments of clarity were few and far between. We had conversations, of course, but he was generally distracted or lost in his mania. Conversations were always one-sided and involved a lot of shouting. His deafness was an added challenge to the whole situation.

When my mother called to announce my father had passed, I did not cry. I didn't feel anything, actually, and those people with whom I shared this detail struggled to understand my lack of emotion. Yet to me it made all the sense in the world. I didn't lose my father on June 4, 2020; I lost my father years ago. Only a shell of who he was remained on the day he died.

In the hell we currently live in, with Covid 19 and an indifferent government led by a president he hated, he may be better off. No more pain, or suffering, or struggling with the little things in life.

But now that I write this memory, I realize I have one regret.

During my father's internment at the convalescent hospital, after the facility went through a hellish month due to a Covid outbreak, you had to call a nurse's station to talk to a patient. I probably didn't try as much as I should have and the one time, I connected I had to leave a message. For the remainder of the day I made sure the ringer on my cellphone was all the way up and the phone near me. But I missed the call.

I missed the last call my father made to me.

In my mind I never succeeded at being a *good son*. When my parents lived nearby, in California, I did not visit as often as I could. I didn't call as much. And when they moved to Phoenix, I had an easy excuse.

And while I can accept that I am left with unanswered questions and I can accept that I should have spent more time with my father, I cannot accept that I missed that last call. That will stick.

Fathers are a challenge to their sons. They are a tremendous influence, sometimes positive and other times, not so much, but the impact remains. Poetry has always helped me get through the pain of life and nothing has changed with the process of surviving crazy.

As long as I live, and continue to write, the story will never be over. His voice is in everything I put down. And that is something, in the end.

epilogue

My father passed away in early June, 2020. He did not know I had plans to write this book. I didn't either.

Writing has long been my outlet to survive what the world throws my way and, admittedly, I have had a normal life without great challenge. Until my father's diagnosis of cancer and dementia.

I made peace with the fact that my father would die two years ago and as his mental illness grew progressively worse, I found myself looking inward more frequently. Many of the poems herein are reflections of that introspection.

Turns out there were behind-the-scenes forces that brought attention to my writing. I found out well after the fact that **Jack Varnell** had been one of these forces. When **Puma Perl** told me that **Punk Hostage Press** had an interest I jumped at the chance. **Punk Hostage Press** has published so many great writers over the years and that I would be included is nothing more than the most incredible honor. And, Subsequently, Puma's delicate editor eye greatly improved my work. Without her assistance this book would not exist, on a number of levels. I also need to thank **Iris Berry** for giving me this opportunity and her unbending patience. She gave me that kick in the ass I needed to finish. Last, but not least, my radio partner in crime, **Rob Plath** who spurred me on and actually gave me the prompt to revisit my childhood.

But the greatest impact on my writing has always been my father. He had expressed an interest in writing when I was a kid but never really did anything about it, which surprised me. He was a voracious reader and could consumer a book in a single sitting if the words captured him. In everything I did he encouraged me, even when he didn't "get" me or the form I chose to express myself. He was always there, whether I knew it or not.

It is to my father I dedicate this book.

I also want to give thanks to a great many editors that rejected my work over the years. It is a silent push I always needed. A sort of fuck you, as my revenge.

A number of presses and related editors have been overly generous to me: **Winamop, Lit Up, Red Fez, Horror Sleaze Trash, Raven Cage, Fearless,** the mad editor himself **John Patrick Robbins,** George Anderson at **Bold Monkey, Cajun Mutt Press,** and so many others.

A special thanks to **Dale Winslow** for her initial read of the manuscript and some very pointed commentary that helped push me.

Many thanks and mad respect to all,

jck
jun 2021

more about the author

In Driving w/ Crazy, Jack Henry takes us on an unflinching journey through a life spent in the shadows of mental illness. Henry's lens is tightly focused on his relationship with his father, who suffered a psychotic break while Henry was only thirteen and was ultimately stricken with cancer and dementia. This is a poetic memoir, composed of beautifully raw, vulnerable pieces, sometimes lyrical, sometimes conversational, but always forthright in their depiction of how both physical and mental illness impacts an entire family, across generations. From tender reminiscences about his L.A. childhood in the 70s and 80s through the present-day Covid-19 crisis, we feel Henry's rage, his helplessness and despair. Together with him, we face our own immortality. But Henry also offers us hope—in seeking to understand the senseless, he uncovers small epiphanies. Sometimes, that's all there is; sometimes, that's enough.

Lauren Scharhag, author *Requiem for a Robot Dog*, (Cajun Mutt Press) and *Languages, First and Last* (Cyberwit.net)

In Jack Henry's moving collection, Driving with Crazy, a boy senses that there is something "missing, something not quite right." As a passenger in his father's car, he realizes the drive will never end. Later, he wonders if a teenager can drive a father mad. Madness is the quiet wind rustling through these contemplative poems. In them, Henry so masterfully, takes us on the life-ride that is the relationship between a father and son. How men become boys and boys become men and how our vulnerabilities unite us. Jack Henry's poetry cuts to the chase never leaving anything behind.

Nicca Ray, author, *Ray by Ray: A Daughter's Take on the Legend of Nicholas Ray* and the poetry collection, *Back Seat Baby*

With a tough but compassionate lens, Jack Henry explores the changing landscape of human nature and relationships. He confidently takes the wheel and drives the reader on a sometimes savage, often spiritual, trip examining love, endurance, loss, and the inevitability of life. Henry's biting poetic revelations are a potent map bringing the reader to a bittersweet and wise destination."

Dale Winslow, Publisher, *NeoPoesis Press*

Jack Henry is a writer/publisher/editor based in Southeastern California and has been an announcer on the Blogtalk Radio show **Rob&Jack America**, publisher of **Heroin Love Songs**, and editor in charge at **d/e/a/d/b/e/a/t press.** In late 2009 Jack started to gain acceptance with a variety of on-line and print lit zines. Several chapbooks followed as well as two full-length collections, "With the Patience of Monuments (NeoPoesis Press) and "Crunked" (Epic Rites Press).

After a 9-year hiatus from all things writing Jack returned in late 2019 to the small press world.

"Driving w/Crazy," from **PUNK HOSTAGE PRESS**, is Jack's first full length publication in 12 years.

additional titles from Punk Hostage Press

Danny Baker
Fractured (2012)
A Razor
Better Than a Gun in A Knife Fight (2012)
Drawn Blood: Collected Works
From D.B.P.LTD., 1985-1995 (2012)
Beaten Up Beaten Down (2012)
Small Catastrophes in A Big World (2012)
Half- Century Status (2013)
Days of Xmas Poems (2014)
Puro Purismo (2021)
Iris Berry
The Daughters of Bastards (2012)
All That Shines Under the Hollywood Sign (2019)
C.V. Auchterlonie
Impress (2012) by
Yvonne De la Vega
Tomorrow, Yvonne - Poetry & Prose for Suicidal Egoists (2012)
Carolyn Srygley- Moore
Miracles Of the Blog: A Series (2012) by
Rich Ferguson
8th & Agony (2012)
Jack Grisham
Untamed (2013)
Code Blue: A Love Story ~ Limited Edition (2014)
Dennis Cruz
Moth Wing Tea (2013)
The Beast Is We (2018)
Frank Reardon
*Blood Music (*2013)
Pleasant Gehman
Showgirl Confidential (2013)
Joel Landmine
Yeah, Well... (2014)

additional titles from Punk Hostage Press

SB Stokes
  History Of Broken Love Things (2014)
Michele McDannold
  Stealing The Midnight from A Handful of Days (2014)
Hollie Hardy
  How To Take a Bullet and Other Survival Poems (2014)
S.A. Griffin
  Dreams Gone Mad with Hope (2014)
A.D. Winans
  Dead Lions (2014)
Nadia Bruce- Rawlings
  Scars (2014)
  Driving in The Rain (2020)
Lee Quarnstrom.
  *WHEN I WAS A DYNAMITER, Or, how a Nice Catholic Boy
  Became a Merry Prankster, a Pornographer, and a Bridegroom Seven Times*
  (2014)
Alexandra Naughton
  I Will Always Be Your Whore/Love Songs For Billy Corgan (2014)
  You Could Never Objectify Me More Than I've Already Objectified Myself
  (2015)
Maisha Z Johnson
  No Parachutes to Carry Me Home (2015) by
Michael Marcus
  #1 Son and Other Stories (2017)
Danny Garcia
  LOOKING FOR JOHNNY, The Legend of Johnny Thunders (2018)
William S. Hayes
  Burden Of Concrete (2020)
Todd Moore
  Dillinger's Thompson (2020)
Dan Denton
  *$100-A-Week Motel (*2021)

www.ingramcontent.com/pod-product-compliance
Lightning Source LLC
Chambersburg PA
CBHW020938090426
42736CB00010B/1188